LIONEL MESSI

★ ALL ACCESS ★

Emma Carlson Berne

Scholastic Inc.

If you purchased this book without a cover, you should be aware that this book is stolen property. It was reported as "unsold and destroyed" to the publisher, and neither the author nor the publisher has received any payment for this "stripped book."

Copyright © 2025 by Scholastic Inc.

All rights reserved. Published by Scholastic Inc., *Publishers since 1920*. SCHOLASTIC and associated logos are trademarks and/or registered trademarks of Scholastic Inc.

The publisher does not have any control over and does not assume any responsibility for author or third-party websites or their content.

No part of this publication may be reproduced, stored in a retrieval system, or transmitted in any form or by any means, electronic, mechanical, photocopying, recording, or otherwise, or used to train any artificial intelligence technologies, without written permission of the publisher. For information regarding permission, write to Scholastic Inc., Attention: Permissions Department, 557 Broadway, New York, NY 10012.

This unauthorized biography was carefully researched to make sure it's accurate. This book is not sponsored by or affiliated with Mr. Messi or anyone involved with him.

Photos Credits: Cover: Mark J. Terrill/AP Images, cnythzl/Getty Images, ulimi/Getty Images, Astrolounge/Getty Images, vkulieva/Getty Images, Saramix/Shutterstock, thebaikers/ Shutterstock, Nikolaeva/Shutterstock, ulimi/Getty Images, Farferros/Shutterstock. Insert 1: Marcelo Boeri/El Grafico/Getty Images, DANIEL GARCIA/AFP/Getty Images, Matt Roberts/Offside/Getty Images. 2: Pressefoto Ulmer\ullstein bild/Getty Images. 3: Abaca Press / Alamy Stock Photo, Shaun Botterill/Getty Images, Gabriel Rossi/LatinContent/ Getty Images. 4: Marc Gonzalez Aloma/Europa Press/Getty Images, Matthias Hangst/ Getty Images. 5: Simon Bruty/Anychance/Getty Images, Pablo Morano/BSR Agency/ Getty Images. 6: David Ramos - FIFA/FIFA/Getty Images. 7: David Ramos - FIFA/FIFA/ Getty Images, Arturo Jimenez/Anadolu Agency/Getty Images. 8: Mike Ehrmann/Getty Images, Pascal Le Segretain/Getty Images..

ISBN 978-1-5461-5427-3

10 9 8 7 6 5 4 3 2 1   25 26 27 28 29

Printed in U.S.A.   40
First printing January 2025

Series design by Sarah Salomon for The Story Division
Cover and photo insert design by Lynne Yeamans and Nancy Leonard for The Story Division

TABLE OF CONTENTS

CHAPTER 1: *A Man, a Ball, a Plan*   1

CHAPTER 2: *Becoming Leo*   12

CHAPTER 3: *A Home at Barça*   24

CHAPTER 4: *Rise to Dominance*   39

CHAPTER 5: *Leo Down, Leo Up*   50

CHAPTER 6: *Leaving Home*   56

CHAPTER 7: *Leo's Big Moment*   64

CHAPTER 8: *The GOAT Forever*   76

CHAPTER 1

A Man, a Ball, a Plan

In a packed stadium in Qatar, a left footer in a blue-striped jersey is about to give a gift to the gods—and the fans—of soccer. The 2022 World Cup final game was in its twenty-third minute. Argentina, with its great soccer star Leo Messi, was pitted against France and its champion player, Kylian Mbappé. The score was 0–0. French player Ousmane Dembélé had fouled Argentine player Ángel Di María. That meant Argentina would get to take a penalty kick. They would have one open shot at the goal, with only the goalie between the ball and the net.

Everyone knew there was only one player who should take this penalty kick. Lionel Messi, the thirty-five-year-old phenomenon who had carried his World Cup team all the way to this moment.

Leo took his place on the field. The referee placed the ball on the white spot marking its place. Twelve yards away, in front of the goal, French goalkeeper Hugo Lloris, clad in all yellow, danced, arms partly extended, ready to throw himself in front of Leo's missile—er, *ball*. In front of the ball, Leo stared down at the grass with his hands on his hips. He breathed deeply, blowing out his cheeks. Every fiber in him was focused on this moment.

He spat, then raised his head. Lloris danced, poised. Then the red-shirted ref held his arm out to the side and blew his whistle.

Leo ran forward, and with arms out to the side, for an instant, faked a little to the left. In that moment, Lloris read his false cue and

threw his body in that direction, across the goal, leaving the net open on the right side. Leo slammed the ball into the net as Lloris hit the ground on the other side of the goal, and Leo took off in a victory sprint across the field as the supporters' cheers rocked the stadium.

Leo fell to the ground in celebration as his teammates tackled him in a joyous dogpile. They were ahead 1–0 and already their chances of clinching a World Cup title were looking up—thanks to Leo.

The Argentine team members weren't the only ones celebrating that night. All over the world, soccer fans were sending up a little prayer of thanks that Leo Messi walks this earth. After all, the man is one of the greatest players in the history of soccer, racking up top awards and trophies like they're pebbles he's picking up off the ground, scoring more than eight hundred career goals.

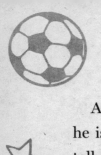

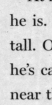

At first, Leo doesn't seem like the über star he is. He's short, only five feet, seven inches tall. On the field, during breaks in the play, he's calm, often strolling around or hanging near the ball. He doesn't seem all that interested in the fact that millions of eyes are watching him.

But Leo isn't uninterested or bored. He's thinking, analyzing, making a mental map of where the ball is—and more importantly, where he wants it to go. And then, when it's time—and not a second before—Leo transforms himself into a blaze of tumbling, switching, dancing action, with the ball glued to his cleats as if by magic.

But Lionel Messi is more than a soccer-ball spell caster. He's a steady, no-drama man whose idea of a perfect day is walking his three kids to school, then drinking tea with his wife. He's a guy who loves his mom so much he once got a yellow card for holding up a birthday

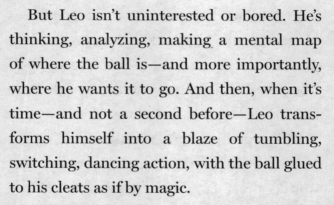

sign for her while on the field. He's Leo Messi, and he won't be put in a box—except the one that's meant for the soccer GOAT.

Soccer School

Soccer? Football? *Association* football? Huh? Soccer may be "the beautiful game," but it doesn't mean it's always easy to understand. Get ready for your first class in soccer school!

 Mainly, it's football—and not the NFL. Soccer is known as "football" in almost every country in the world, including South America and Europe. Just a few countries call the game "soccer"—mainly, the United States, Canada, Australia, New Zealand, and South Africa.

 Association football—*what?* This strange term was created by the British in the mid-1800s. Later, people started calling the game "soc," from "association." Eventually, "soc" became . . . you guessed it . . . "soccer."

⚽ Medieval people in England played a version of soccer—often with villages competing between each other. Sometimes teams had hundreds of players—and the goals might be several miles apart. Yes, that's right, miles. Punching and fighting were allowed.

⚽ Soccer is the most popular sport in the world and is played in almost every country on Earth! About 240 million people are registered players, but casual players number in the billions.

⚽ Professional soccer players run an average of seven miles during a game—except for goalies. They move the least.

⚽ There are eleven total positions in soccer, grouped into four basic areas (goalkeeper, defender, midfield, and attack). Leo plays forward for Inter Miami, which is an attack position.

FUN FACT

Leo runs plenty on the field. But he also walks when on the field, too—an average of three miles per game.

THESE ARE A FEW OF HIS FAVORITE THINGS

No brown paper packages tied up with string here, though.

- ⚽ Order and routine at home. "Before going to sleep, I like to leave the table ready for the next morning. During breakfast, everyone is always in their place, in the same place," Leo told the Spanish newspaper *Marca*.

- ⚽ His wife. Leo says he admires "everything" about her!

- ⚽ Argentine reggae, Mexican pop music from the band Grupo Frontera, and songs by Puerto Rican rapper Bad Bunny and Columbian singer Karol G—all from his Apple music warm-up playlist.

- ⚽ A shoeless house. "When I get home, I take off my shoes right away and if I'm confident with others I also do it at their home," Leo has said.

⚽ Cars! Leo has a great collection of cars, including a Ferrari 335 S Spider Scaglietti and a Bentley Bentayga.

⚽ Favorite sports other than soccer? Tennis, basketball, the racquet sport padel, and American football. "I am learning a lot about American football and have come to understand it more and I am enjoying it," Leo has said.

⚽ Walking his kids to school. Leo tries to do this dad task each day before coming back home to spend time with his wife.

LEO IN UNIFORM

Stripes, checks, pink, red, black, blue—
Leo brings class to all the uniforms he's
worn over the years.

- Leo started his career in the red-with-black-checks jersey of the Newell's Old Boys.

- Blue-and-red stripes with yellow trimmings were Leo's colors for his seventeen years with FC Barcelona.

- Leo donned blue with red trimmings for his brief stint with Paris Saint-Germain.

- Leo wears a stylish pink jersey with a collar for his time on the field for Inter Miami CF.

CHAPTER 2

Becoming Leo

At first, he wasn't Leo. He was Lionel and he was born on June 24, 1987, in Rosario, Argentina. Rosario was one of the largest cities in Argentina and it supported not one but two professional soccer teams. It kind of had to—soccer was *the* sport of regular people in Argentina. No, in South America. Actually, in the whole world. But in Rosario, wealthy people might play polo or rugby. But on the streets and the little fields scattered among the neighborhoods, it was soccer, always soccer.

Leo's parents, Jorge and Celia, already had two sons, Rodrigo and Mathias, by the time Leo came along. Jorge was a supervisor at a steel manufacturing plant. Celia worked in a shop that sold magnetic coils. The family lived in a comfortable two-story home, and Leo grew up surrounded by the love and support of his parents and his grandmother, Celia.

Leo was small, quiet, and serious. He did his schoolwork and his homework and tried not to draw attention to himself at school. But as soon as he could walk, Leo's attention was on one thing: the soccer ball. He was obsessed. He carried a ball with him everywhere, even to bed. By the time he was four, he was playing with his brothers and his cousins in the street, on the local playing field, anywhere they could find. His dad would coach games on the local field. During one game, when the ball was elsewhere on the field, Leo started dribbling with stones lying on the ground while he waited for his chance to dribble with the real thing.

Grandma Insists

Leo's brothers already played on the local youth team, Newell's Old Boys, along with his cousins. But Leo wasn't interested in joining a club team. He liked to just play on the street with the neighborhood kids. Still, Leo and his parents and grandmother walked to the field most days to watch the practices. One day, during one of his older brother's games, Leo was goofing around on the sidelines with a soccer ball while his mother and grandmother watched the game. The coach, Salvador Aparicio, saw him dribbling the ball by himself. Coach Aparicio was one player short for the game. And this boy was incredibly young—younger than all the players—and

very small. Really small, actually. But also? Really good. Really, *really* good, actually.

Coach Aparicio asked Leo's mother and grandmother if he could play in the game—or actually, Leo remembers that his grandmother *insisted* he play in the game. "Put him, put him!" Leo recalled his grandmother saying.

Coach Aparicio put him in. And Leo didn't even know what to do, really. When the ball rolled by him, he just stood there. But then, the second time the ball rolled by, something activated Leo. He kicked the ball—and his soccer career began.

Leo was too small to even shoot the ball in that game, but that didn't matter. Coach Aparicio could see that he was brilliant beyond brilliant. Leo's grandmother told the coach to buy Leo some cleats. If the coach would do that, she'd bring Leo back to practice.

And she did. After that, Leo's grandmother walked him to every practice and stood on the sidelines, watching. When he was only eight, Leo could already keep the ball just under his cleat when he dribbled and cut sideways, and could even bend the ball into the corners.

Medical Problems

But Leo was still very short and small. In fact, he was so unusually small that when he was ten, his parents finally took him to the doctor. There, he was diagnosed with a growth hormone deficiency. This meant his body wasn't making enough of the hormone it needed to get bigger and taller. The doctors studied Leo for a year and by the time he was eleven, they realized he had hardly grown at all. He would need treatment.

Every day, Leo would have to inject himself with shots of human growth hormone in his thighs. He would alternate legs so his muscles

could rest. Soon, Leo's legs were covered in scars and puncture marks.

And the injections were expensive. They cost about nine hundred dollars a month. Jorge and Celia and their children had a comfortable, middle-class life, and they had health insurance, but Leo needed the injections for three years. Leo's parents calculated that they could afford only two years of shots.

Jorge and Celia didn't know what to do. Leo needed someone to help cover the cost of his injections. The family couldn't afford it. The Old Boys couldn't afford it. And other clubs in Argentina thought Leo was too small to consider as a future player. He had to keep getting the treatments if he wanted to play serious soccer.

Then, Leo's luck changed. He and his parents had already been in touch with two football representatives named Fabian Soldini

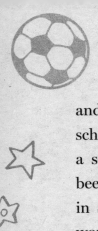

and Martin Montero, who had a football school in Rosario. Fabian and Martin knew a sports agent, Horacio Gaggioli, who had been born in Argentina but was now based in Spain. They wanted to know if Horacio would be interested in checking out this new, very small, very amazing soccer phenom from Rosario. Horacio was interested, very much. And when he did, Horacio wasted no time organizing a tryout for Leo with the famed club FC Barcelona.

In September 2000, Leo and his dad packed up and boarded a plane for Spain. They were going to Barcelona. Leo's grandmother Celia had died two years before. But her football dreams for her grandson were already becoming a reality.

ALL ABOUT ARGENTINA

- Argentina's favorite sport—after soccer, of course? Polo! Players mounted on specially trained horses charge up and down a field the length of nine American football fields, trying to hit a ball with long mallets. The horses can reach speeds of up to forty miles per hour!

- Argentineans also play a polo-basketball mashup called "pato." Riders on horseback gallop up and down a field, trying to throw a ball with handles through a hoop. When the game was first invented, players used a dead bird wrapped in a leather bag instead of a ball.

- In 1986, when Argentina won the World Cup, several hundred thousand screaming fans poured outside, blocking streets with cars and trucks. But even that celebration couldn't compare to the 2022 celebration when so many people partied that a parade had to be canceled, and the players had to fly in helicopters over the crowd.

 Soccer was brought to Argentina in the mid-1800s by British sailors. They would play casual games while waiting at the docks, and local Argentineans would watch. In 1931, Argentina created its first professional team—and a national obsession took hold.

 Tennis is another Argentine fave, mostly played by the upper and middle classes. Argentine players have won the French Open, the US Open, and (once) the finals of Wimbledon.

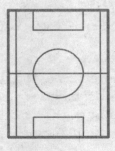

GREATEST SOCCER PLAYERS OF ALL TIME

Leo has some competition for his title of Soccer GOAT!

 Pelé—born into poverty in Brazil in 1940, Pelé is considered by many to be the greatest soccer player ever (hmm, what do you think about that, Messi?). He led the Brazilian national team to three World Cup titles and was FIFA's co-Player of the Century in 1999.

 Diego Maradona—Messi had competed with the legacy of this Argentine legend his entire career. And rightly so—Maradona led his club team to championships around the world and the national team to the 1986 World Cup win.

Ronaldo—not to be confused with Cristiano Ronaldo, this soccer legend carried his team to the 2002 World Cup win and nailed down three FIFA Player of the Year Awards.

 Johan Cruyff—this Dutch player also played for FC Barcelona, like the legend who would follow in his tracks. Cruyff played with the Dutch national team in the 1974 World Cup where his quick change of direction on the pitch (leaving his defender looking at thin air) became known as the "Cruyff Turn."

FUN FACT

When he was younger, Leo idolized legendary Argentine player Pablo Aimar. Pablo even offered a seventeen-year-old Leo his jersey after a game in 2004.

CHAPTER 3

A Home at Barça

For two weeks, Leo was on trial at FC Barcelona. The first game the club arranged was between Leo and kids his own age, and opposing them, kids from the next age bracket up. From the moment Leo started playing, the ball was glued to his foot. The agent Horacio Gaggioli remembers, "Lionel stood out straightaway. He touched the ball like no one else. There were nerves, but Lionel soon dispelled them."

Leo was clearly a special talent, but not everyone was convinced FC Barcelona—

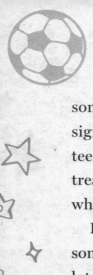

sometimes called Barça by its fans—should sign him. For one thing, he was only thirteen! And he needed all this special medical treatment. He was so small and skinny—what if he didn't grow?

Barça told Jorge and Leo that they needed some time to think. The club didn't have a lot of money right then—in fact, they were almost bankrupt—and they weren't sure they wanted to spend on a new contract for this small phenom. Leo and his dad flew back to Argentina without a promise from the team.

By December, Leo and his parents were getting nervous. Barça still had not given them an answer, though the club directors and Leo's representatives were talking. Finally, Jorge told Leo's representatives that if Barça didn't give them a promise, Leo was going to go somewhere else.

Promise on a Napkin

The club directors didn't want to lose out on this chance, even though Leo was young, small, and his contract would be expensive. One night, the club director, Charly Rexach, was having dinner with Leo's representatives. They were all talking to Jorge on the phone and Jorge was getting upset. He demanded that Barça give them some proof that they were going to sign Leo. Charly could see that he needed to give Jorge a written promise, right then and there, and so he asked the waiter for a paper napkin and a pen. On the napkin, he wrote, "In Barcelona, on 14 December 2000 and in the presence of Messrs Minguella and Horacio, Carles Rexach, FC Barcelona's sporting director, hereby agrees, under his responsibility and regardless of any dissenting opinions, to sign the player Lionel Messi, provided that we keep to the amounts agreed upon." Then he signed his name.

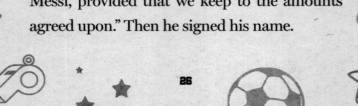

It may have been on a napkin, but Leo Messi officially had his first soccer contract.

Leo, his parents, and his two brothers and one sister all packed up their lives, uprooted themselves from Rosario, and moved to Barcelona in February 2001 so Leo could join the FC Barcelona youth team. He was thirteen.

But the move was hard. Leo lived in an apartment with his family, instead of in the dorms with the rest of the youth players. So, he didn't have as much of a chance to make friends. He did have one, who remembered later riding the bus with Messi. "I remember clearly, as if it was yesterday, us both sitting there with a Discman in our hand. Leo loved telling me about his life in Argentina, and his Discman was full of cumbia songs (traditional South American music). He'd play them for me all the time, and I'd do the same for him with Spanish music," Toronto footballer Víctor Vázquez told an interviewer years later.

But Leo was lonely. He struggled with ankle injuries, and his family was having a hard time adjusting to Barcelona. They missed their life in Argentina. His mother was especially unhappy. She missed the open spaces of Rosario—Barcelona felt too busy and too cramped. Gradually, the Messi family began splitting up. First, Leo's two big brothers left Spain and went home to Argentina. Then, Leo's parents realized that the move had been too hard for his little sister, who was only five years old at the time. Leo's mom would return to Rosario with her, they decided. Leo and Jorge would stay on in Barcelona.

Leo was homesick without his mom. He missed her terribly and he missed home. For three years, he would only see her every four months. He cried every time he had to get on the plane to return to Barcelona after a visit. In the locker room, he was silent. He would sit

in a corner and not speak, and after the practice was over, he'd take a shower and leave as fast as he could.

Missing Home, Loving the Game

But he had his dad, and the two of them spent a lot of time together eating takeout and playing video games in their small apartment near the Barça training grounds. "It was very tough for me," Leo told *Sports Illustrated* many years later. "There were moments when I was really sad and homesick, but I never thought of leaving. I knew I wanted to stay and keep playing."

By 2002, Leo started playing in matches—and feeling a lot better. He began traveling with the youth team. He even got officially hazed when the other players took everything out of his hotel room one night—when they told him they did that to all new players, Leo knew he was part of the team now. In October 2004, Leo made his official debut with the team as a sub.

But on May 1, 2005, Leo put on the number 30 jersey with red-and-blue stripes and exploded into the professional soccer world when he scored his first official goal in a match against Spanish team FC Albacete.

The game was already in its eighty-seventh minute when Messi was brought in off the bench as a substitute. The seventeen-year-old sprinted onto the field and play began. Three minutes after he'd been brought in, Messi got possession of the ball near the penalty box. Then he went to work, dribbling effortlessly past his defenders, keeping control of the ball, then shooting with calm precision past the goalie and into the net. He'd been in the game for four minutes.

But even amid the joy of his first career goal, Leo didn't forget who brought him to this place. He pointed his finger up to the sky to heaven, dedicating the goal to his grandmother Celia.

Leo was on his way—until he wasn't. As he prepared for the 2005 season, he got some bad news. Because he was from Argentina, not the European Union, he wasn't going to be allowed to keep playing for his league. There were only three spots in the club for players from non-European Union countries, and those spots were already taken by other players. When he joined FC Barcelona way back when he was thirteen, Leo and his dad had assumed he'd be considered an "adopted" European Union player because he was so young. But no, Leo was told now in 2005. He was not, and under league rules, he could not play.

But Leo's great-grandfather had been born in a region of Spain. Leo could get Spanish citizenship, and soon after his eligibility problem, he did. Leo was now a citizen of two countries—Argentina and Spain—he was cleared to play—and FC Barcelona—and the world—was ready to see him on the field.

MESSI'S BEST FITS

Leo's moves on the field are plenty fancy—but sometimes he brings the fancy to his off-field life, too.

- Leo sparkled in a sequined black tux at the 2021 Ballon d'Or awards. And the icing on the cake? His three sons wore sparkly tuxes to match their dad's!

- Leo also keeps it casual in graphic hoodies from his own fashion line.

- At the 2014 Ballon d'Or, Leo mixed it up with an unconventional tux in a glittery wine red.

- A giant white T-shirt and baggy navy shorts are a classic Messi combo.

Polka dots? Yes, please! Leo got playful with a white polka dot jacket and matching bow tie at the 2013 Ballon d'Or.

 Party time? Also, T-shirt time. Leo puts on a black graphic T-shirt, baggy black pants, and black-and-white sneakers for a night out with Antonela.

TALKING ABOUT MESSI: BEST QUOTES ABOUT LEO

⚽ "It is clear that Messi is above all others. Those who do not see that are blind."
—Xavi, former teammate

⚽ "Messi for the last three or four years has been the best player in the world—he has been at a level of consistency I don't think the world has seen before."
—Cristiano Ronaldo (you already know who he is!)

⚽ "He was probably more eye-catching at twenty-two when he dribbled past even his own shadow. Now, this latest version of him makes him the best of all; he does everything he has to, whenever he has to do it."
—Pablo Aimar, former teammate

"I like Messi a lot, he's a great player. Technically, we're practically at the same level."
—Pelé, Brazilian soccer legend

"Messi continues to show it doesn't matter your size, it just matters how good your football brain is."
—Dwayne De Rosario, former Canadian player

"You are in our hearts and we have never seen you play in our country."
—Alberto Fernandez, president of Argentina

"This Barça will be remembered as Messi's Barça. He's well above anything else I've ever seen. He's an alien."
—Carles Puyol, former teammate

"I had never seen anything like it. He did incredible things for a kid his age—the same things he still does match after match now, but at that size. He was not only a spectacular player, but he managed to have the ball continuously."
—Carles Rexach, Messi's first technical director at FC Barcelona

"I have seen the player who will inherit my place in Argentine football and his name is Messi. Messi is a genius."
—Diego Maradona, Argentine soccer legend

 "This is one of the greatest players in the world."
—David Beckham, British soccer star

 "You know, I think that Messi guy might have a future."
—Joe Biden, president of the United States

FUN FACT

Leo's never been a tall man. In fact, his height of five foot, seven inches makes him two inches shorter than the average American man.

CHAPTER 4

Rise to Dominance

Leo was a Spaniard now and FC Barcelona was his club, but he was also and always an Argentinean and a member of the Argentina national team. In 2006, at the age of only eighteen, Leo took his team, his heart, and his left foot to Germany for the biggest soccer match on the planet—the World Cup.

On June 16, 2006, Argentina took the field against Serbia and Montenegro in the second stage of their World Cup bid. Argentina scored three goals in the first seventy-three minutes of the game, leaving Serbia and

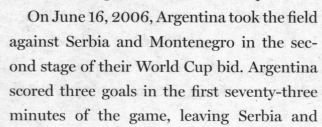

Montenegro with zero. Leo Messi sat on the bench—he was only a sub. But in the seventy-fourth minute, he became much more.

With the Argentine team safely ahead, the manager could afford to send in some subs—and Leo, wearing number 19, was called off the bench to replace his teammate Maxi Rodríguez. "The Boy Wonder is about to enter the World Cup," the announcer declared. "Lionel Messi, just eighteen years old . . . Lionel Messi becomes the youngest Argentina player to play the World Cup since 1934."

Leo stood up and breathed deep. His face was focused and intent. He ran onto the field and found the ball, lightly weaving through his defenders. Then, in the eighty-eighth minute, Leo's teammate Carlos Tevez slipped the ball to Leo, who was ready and took it up like it was glued to his foot. Lightly, leaving a defender sprawling in front of him, Leo flew

down the field and shot the ball into the net as the goalie sprawled helplessly in front of it. He made it look as easy as a day on the kids' field in Rosario.

Over the next three years, Leo would lead FC Barcelona to three different league titles and receive his first FIFA Player of the Year Award—and in 2009, Leo stood in a suit and tie on a stage in Paris and accepted the gold soccer ball that was the Ballon d'Or—the top individual soccer award in Europe. Leo was the first Argentine player to receive this honor.

Messi Must

But out there on Planet Soccer, Leo had a rival. The year before, in 2008, the Portuguese superstar Cristiano Ronaldo had won the Ballon d'Or. Cristiano was only two years older than Leo. Like Leo, he was one of the greatest players alive. Fans started asking:

Who was better? Messi or Ronaldo? One was flashy, one was serious. They were head-to-head in goals, assists, and awards. But neither player trashed the other to the media. Instead, fans took that on for them, declaring their allegiance for one player or the other.

The 2014 World Cup final could prove Leo's dominance. He'd never won a Cup yet, and in the soccer world, he had to snare that trophy to truly be vaulted into the ranks of GOAT players. Argentina had staggered through the different stages as the tournament went on, not playing very well, but gradually beating out rival after rival, mostly due to Leo, who had scored four goals for his team throughout.

Now Leo fans had their eyes fixed on the field as Argentina faced Germany in the final game. The score was 0–0 and Leo hadn't scored—no one had scored. Leo had missed a couple of easy goals, and the feeling on the field was grim. The regulation time of ninety

minutes ended with the score *still* tied at 0–0. The game went into overtime. The teams would have a thirty-minute period of playing time. The team ahead at the end of the thirty minutes would be the winner.

The whistle blew for overtime and the clock began ticking down. Twenty-two minutes of scoreless play and then, in the twenty-third minute, German player Mario Götze sent the ball into the net, bringing the score to 1–0. Seven minutes left in overtime and Argentina *must* score to tie the game—or lose the World Cup. Then the chance came. Leo was set up for a free kick. This meant he would get one free shot at the goal. "The little boy from Rosario, Argentina, on behalf of every little boy wearing his shirt," British commentator Peter Drury said as Messi placed the ball on the free kick spot. "Messi on a million backs. Messi for a million flashbulbs. One kick of the ball."

The tension in the stadium twanged like a guitar string. Leo backed up from the ball. He ran his hand over his hair, then over his face. "Messi must," Peter Drury intoned from the press box. Leo wiped his face on his jersey.

Then, he ran forward, his body tilted into a sprint, his eyes on the ball. He kicked and the ball soared—too high, sailing over the goalpost by six inches, as Peter Drury cried, "No, no, no!" echoing the hearts of every Argentina fan on earth that night.

The whistle blew, signaling the end of the game—the end of the World Cup. Argentina had lost. Leo's face was etched with gloom, even as he accepted the Golden Ball trophy for most valuable tournament player.

Comfort at Home

But Leo had the best fan club waiting for him at home—his girlfriend, Antonela, and their

two-year-old son, Thiago. Leo met Antonela in Rosario when he was nine years old (!) and she was only eight. Leo was spending the summer at his friend Lucas's house. Soon, he met Lucas's cousin—a girl named Antonela Roccuzzo. After the summer was over, Leo wrote Antonela letters—and she became his girlfriend. When Leo had to leave for Barcelona, he stayed in touch with Antonela, even flying home to be with her when her best friend died in a car crash.

Leo revealed his relationship with Antonela to the world in 2009 when he told a soccer news show that he had a girlfriend and that she was in Argentina. Soon, photos of the pair in bathing suits in Rio showed up in the media, and before long, Antonela had left Argentina behind and moved her life to Spain to live with Leo in Barcelona. In 2015, Leo's second son, Mateo, was born. He didn't have a World Cup trophy—yet—but Leo had already won an even better prize—his loving family.

HE'S A GOOD BOY

Leo learned kindness growing up in his loving family—and now he likes to keep it going.

- Leo loves his mom so much he once got a fine and a yellow card for lifting up his jersey after scoring a goal to show an undershirt that said, "Happy Birthday, Mami!"

- Leo started a foundation in 2007 to help protect the health and safety of kids around the world. The foundation has worked with UNICEF (the United Nations Children's Fund) to help build water pumps so kids in developing nations can have clean water to drink.

- Messi donates his own money to help others, too. During the COVID-19 pandemic, he gave one million euros of his own money to support health care in Argentina.

Leo is a UNICEF Goodwill Ambassador, too—he travels with UNICEF to areas of the world that need help and meets people there, to show the world what these areas need and how to help. Leo went to Haiti in 2010 after a terrible earthquake there, to learn how the world could help the children of Haiti.

 Leo and Antonela almost made a fan pass out when they stopped their SUV and motioned Miami fans over to meet Leo and get autographs signed. One fan hyperventilated; she was so excited to meet Leo! (She was fine.)

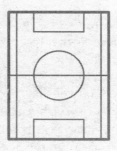

TRAIN LIKE MESSI!

How does the world's greatest player stay that way? Training, training—oh,and training!

- Leo likes to focus on speed in his workouts. He does lunges, hamstring stretches, and squats on his training days. He ends each workout with acceleration drills—basically, running fast in different ways.

- Leo has to stay quick on his feet. He skips over hurdles and cones to train himself to change direction easily.

- But Leo knows that rest is important for his training, too. His trainers make sure he often starts games by sitting on the bench or comes off the field after only an hour. This way, Leo makes sure he can keep playing forever, and ever, and ever . . .

Eating for power—Leo's careful about his diet. He works with a nutritionist who has him eating lots of whole grains, fresh fruits and veggies, olive oil, and of course, plenty of water. Leo eats nuts and seeds, but he has to watch his famous sweet tooth—no sugar!

 But tea? Yes, please! When he's in training, Leo often drinks *mate*, a hot tea loaded with antioxidants and vitamins.

CHAPTER 5

Leo Down, Leo Up

The Leo Messi who walked into the Barcelona Provincial Court in the summer of 2016 looked like a very different Leo than the soccer superstar who dominated the field in a sweaty, shiny jersey and shorts. This Leo was wearing a dark suit and a tie. He had a serious expression on his face. His dad, Jorge, walked beside him, wearing his own dark suit and sunglasses.

Leo and his dad were in trouble. The Spanish Tax Agency—like the United States' IRS—had accused the father and son pair of

hiding over 4 million euros of their money from the tax agency. The tax agency said that Leo and his dad had hidden their money by investing it in companies in countries that have very low taxes. They did not tell the tax agency about this money. This is illegal.

Leo in Trouble

But Leo told the judge that he didn't know any of this was happening. "I don't know about that. All I did was play soccer; I trusted my dad. I never asked about that subject [taxes]. I don't know anything about that, I never had an interest in that, honestly," he told the judge.

In the end, the judge agreed with Leo. He had to pay a fine of 2.25 million euros, but he did not have to go to jail. Leo's dad, Jorge, had to pay a fine of 1.6 million euros.

But Leo was angry about being accused. He said in interviews that he thought about

leaving FC Barcelona, even though he didn't want to. He felt like the Spanish Tax Agency was singling him out and accusing him more harshly than others who had done something similar.

Leo in Love

Leo didn't leave, though, and in 2017, he had a happier event to take his mind off his legal problems—his wedding to Antonela. Back in Rosario, in June, Leo and Antonela were married in a ceremony in a fancy hotel. Antonela wore a sleeveless, lacy dress with a long train and Leo wore a dark suit with a light tie and a big grin. Leo's Barça teammates watched from the audience, along with the Colombian pop star Shakira. Fans crowded barriers outside, craning for photos as police held them back. Inside, the guests ate beef dishes and empanadas, in honor of the pair's Argentine heritage.

Leo had his own family now. He loved the quiet routine he and Antonela had created, and he loved being a dad. "I'm ecstatic about the family we have been able to create. A typical day involves taking Thiago to school, going to training, hanging out at home drinking mate and spending time with Anto and the kids at the park or somewhere. It's a normal, calm life, the kind of life we have always wanted," he told famous soccer journalist Grant Wahl. And soon, Leo and Antonela had their third son, Ciro, in 2018—and Leo's family was complete.

MESSI BY THE NUMBERS

Leo's stats are stratospheric!

 672 goals for FC Barcelona

 778 games for FC Barcelona

 32 goals for Paris Saint-Germain

 74 games for Paris Saint-Germain

 Played in 5 World Cups (only 6 players in the world have done this!)

 Won 1 World Cup

 Worth about $600 million

BEST MESSI MEMES

Sit back, get comfy on the couch, and enjoy this selection of the finest Messi memes.

- Messi: Because scoring one goal is too mainstream!

- Players who played with Leo say Messi is the best. Players who played with Ronaldo also say Messi is the best.

- CR7 (Ronaldo): The god of football sent me to the best!
  Messi: I don't remember sending anyone.

- Blonde or brown, Barça or Argentina, no matter what, Messi remains the best.

- Ronaldo! Call me when you're better than me.

- In Messi's best year, he was compared to Pelé and Maradona. In Ronaldo's best year, he was compared to Messi. The difference!

CHAPTER 6

Leaving Home

Barça was Leo's adopted home for twenty years. It was his family's home, too. For seventeen seasons, Leo had played in red-and-blue stripes in front of thousands of screaming fans on Barça's famous field, Camp Nou. His teammates were like his family. His fans were like his family.

And then in 2021, it all came to an end. FC Barcelona leaders told Leo the news he never thought he would hear. They were not going to renew his contract. Leo's previous salary had been expensive—more than 594 million

dollars over four years. But Leo had already told Barça that he'd agree to a big pay cut to help Barça afford his new contract.

It wasn't enough. Barça was in huge financial trouble. They were already in debt and COVID-19 restrictions had cost them even more money. Leo was released to join a new team.

On August 8, 2021, Leo stood in a blue suit and tie in the FC Barcelona pressroom. "I don't know if I will be able to talk," he said with his eyes full of tears. He paused for a long moment, sniffling and wiping his nose with a tissue. "It is very difficult for me after so many years here. I am not ready to leave."

But he had to leave. And even in his grief, Leo was practical. He was only thirty-four, with many years left in his soccer career. He wanted to keep playing—so he had to find a new club.

A Life in Paris

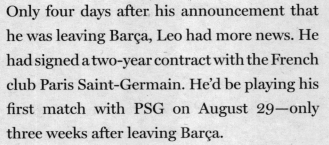

Only four days after his announcement that he was leaving Barça, Leo had more news. He had signed a two-year contract with the French club Paris Saint-Germain. He'd be playing his first match with PSG on August 29—only three weeks after leaving Barça.

But Paris wasn't so great for Leo. He missed Barcelona. Antonela and his kids missed Spain, too. They had trouble adjusting to Paris, just like Leo's own mother and siblings had trouble adjusting to Barcelona so many years earlier. Leo got booed by Barça fans when he was on the field. Even though he won three league trophies for his team, he struggled to bond with the PSG fans.

Leo needed something big. A big win. A World Cup win. And his chance was fast approaching. On November 20, the 2022 World Cup would kick off. Leo would be there, leading the Argentina national team. He was one of the very best players on earth. He'd won almost every award and trophy a soccer player could win. He had played in four World Cups so far. He had never won a title. And he didn't know how many more chances would be in his future.

THE GOAT: LEO'S BROKEN RECORDS

- ⚽ Most goals scored for Argentina in international play
- ⚽ Most goals scored for a South American nation
- ⚽ Youngest Argentinean to score at a World Cup
- ⚽ Most individual World Cup appearances
- ⚽ Most Argentina World Cup goals
- ⚽ Most Ballon d'Or awards
- ⚽ Most goals scored in a club year
- ⚽ 700+ goals in club play

Even as a teenager in 2003, Leo had excellent control of the ball. Here, he dribbles during a photo shoot just before his **FC BARCELONA** debut.

Between matches at his **WORLD CUP** debut, Leo blew bubbles on the sidelines.

In 2006, Leo became the youngest Argentinean to play in the **WORLD CUP**.

Rivals and friends Leo and Cristiano Ronaldo fight for control of the ball in a 2012 match between **BARCELONA** and Real Madrid.

Leo won his first (of eight—and counting) BALLON D'OR awards in 2008, wearing a classic dark suit.

A barefaced young Leo with longer hair celebrates during a 20? game against ARSENA?

Leo and Antonela smile after their 2017 Rosario WEDDING.

"I am here to say goodbye," said an emotional Leo at the press conference announcing his departure from BARCELONA in 2021.

Leo's time in PARIS SAINT-GERMAIN lasted only two seasons.

★ Leo hugs his sons after winning the 2022 WORLD CUP, showing the world just how much he loves them.

FEED THE GOAT

What does the GOAT eat to keep up his energy? His mom's version of a classic Argentine dish tops the list.

- Celia Messi's Milanesa—chicken cutlets breaded, fried, and topped with a tomatoey sauce, ham, and cheese, then baked

- The classic Argentine grilled meat called asada—tons of different meats, all grilled

- Roast chicken with roasted vegetables

- Veal chops

- Eggs and ham

- Beans and rice

- Pasta

Leo also *loves* sweets. He tries to limit them, but among his faves:

- ⚽ Toast with dulce de leche, a sweet, thick, caramel-like sauce made from milk
- ⚽ Chocolate
- ⚽ Ice cream
- ⚽ More dulce de leche

And the NO list! Leo knows he has to eat healthily when he's in training—which is always. He's tried to cut these foods from his diet, even though he loves them:

- ⚽ Pizza—except for cheat days
- ⚽ Red meat (so much for that asada, Leo)
- ⚽ Pork (no asada for you, Leo, again!)
- ⚽ Cheese (oh no! No Mom's Milanesa!)
- ⚽ Fizzy drinks

FUN FACT

Leo likes to collect trophies. He won thirty-five for FC Barcelona during his time with the team, making him the most trophied player in the club's history.

CHAPTER 7

Leo's Big Moment

By December 18, 2022, Leo and his team had clawed their way to the World Cup final. Just one month earlier, Argentina had been defeated 2-1 by Saudi Arabia in the tournament opening match. Now they were facing France and its own superstar, the great player Kylian Mbappé.

Argentina hadn't won a World Cup since 1986. France had just won in 2018. Leo wanted this win. Argentina's fans wanted this win. Perhaps the world wanted this win? Leo would have to see.

Leo's team took the field with aggression when the clock began. Halfway through the first half, Argentina was awarded a penalty kick. It had to go to Leo, who nailed it into the net, scoring the first goal of the game. 1–0 Argentina. Thirty-six minutes into the game, another goal, this time from forward Ángel Di María, who kissed his hands toward the sky as tears of joy filled his eyes. 2–0 Argentina.

They were ahead, but there was still a lot of game left, and Kylian Mbappé knew that. In the eightieth minute, it was Mbappé's turn for the penalty shot, which he slammed into the net, bringing the score to 2–1. Argentina was teetering on the brink, even with a stadium packed with fans in the team's blue-and-white stripes. Then, just a minute and thirty seconds later, it happened again—Mbappé made another goal, bringing the score to 2–2.

The game was tied. The teams fought it out for the rest of game. The buzzer sounded and the game was officially in overtime. Leo scored again—3–2. Then Mbappé scored. 3–3. Overtime ended with the teams still tied— and the World Cup final would be decided in a penalty shoot-out.

It was very simple. Each team would get five shots on the goal. The team who scored the most would win.

Shooting It Out

France sent Mbappé up first. With his face set, the French star ran hard and fast at the ball as Emiliano Martínez, the green-clad goalkeeper, danced in front of the goal. Mbappé fired the ball up and to the left, and Martínez flew at it— and missed. France had scored one penalty kick.

Then it was Argentina's turn. And of course, they sent in—who else?—Leo.

He walked forward calmly as the ref placed the ball on its white spot. He checked the ball.

Then he backed up, his hands on his hips. "In the 1,003rd game of his entire career, the most important kick of his life to date," the Fox announcer said.

Leo stood ready, his head down. The ref blew his whistle. The stadium rumbled with waiting energy.

Then Leo backed up a step and ran in place for an instant, gaining momentum—and ran forward, booting the ball with almost comical ease, as the French goalie fell in front of it—and missed. One penalty kick scored for Argentina.

Back and forth they went, with France kicking and missing, then Argentina kicking and scoring, France kicking and missing, then Argentina scoring again, bringing the total to 3–1 Argentina. France kicked—and scored. 3–2.

If Argentina made one more kick, they'd win. France would not have enough tries left to keep up. Argentina sent Gonzalo Montiel onto the field as Leo and the team lined up to watch, arms over one another's shoulders, faces tense and waiting.

Montiel for the Win

Montiel walked up to position the ball. Eighty-nine thousand fans grew quiet. Montiel backed up and took a deep breath. The ref blew his whistle. Carefully, slowly, Montiel ran forward and shot left—the goalie threw himself right and the ball flew into the net. "Yes!" the announcer shouted as the stadium let loose a tremendous roar and Montiel pulled off his jersey in celebration. He held it over his face as Leo and his teammates tackled him in a joyous, weeping pile.

They had done it. For sixteen years, the golden trophy had slipped out of Leo's grasp. Now, with fireworks exploding in the

background, surrounded by his teammates, Leo hoisted the trophy high above his head, his face lit up with joy. The boy from Rosario had led his team to the World Cup—and to the win.

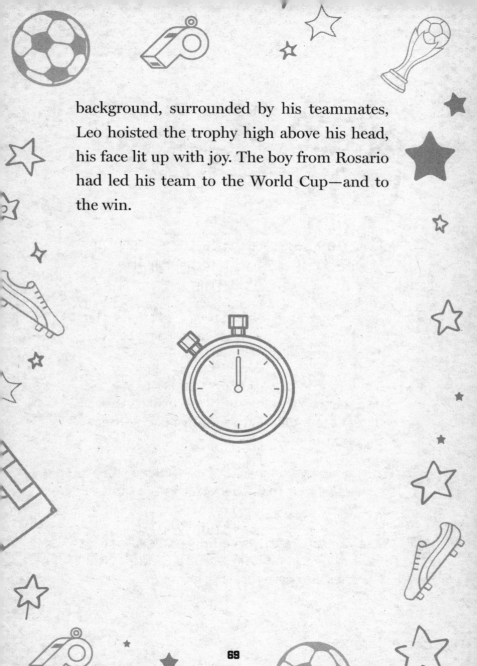

INKED UP: LEO'S TATTOOS

Leo has seventeen tattoos—so far. Read on to find the inspiration behind all this ink.

- Closed and open lotus flowers, symbols that talent can grow anywhere, according to one of Leo's tattooists.

- Crown tattoo on inside of right arm—Antonela has a matching one! Perhaps this is meant to indicate that they're each other's king and queen?

- Enormous eye on inside of right bicep—Leo hasn't said, but many believe this is a picture of Antonela's eye.

- Rose window tattoo on elbow—this one is inspired by the beautiful round windows in churches and cathedrals.

- Jesus on upper arm—Leo declares his firm faith in Christianity with this picture.

- Clock on lower arm—perhaps symbolizing the role of time?

- Clock cogs beneath the clock—these are the gears that help the clock go.

- Rosary beads on arm—both a declaration of Leo's faith and a tribute to his hometown of Rosario.

- His mother's face on his back—this was Leo's very first tattoo—and one of his most special.

- Thiago's handprints and a heart with his name, on the back of his calf—a sign of love for his first son.

- The birthdates of his wife and three sons at the bottom of his left leg—*and* his right.

- And the ex-tattoo—Leo used to have a tattoo of a sword with wings, but he's since had it covered with black ink, and he hasn't said why!

- ⚽ A pair of red lips at the bottom of his stomach—pretty likely these are meant to be Antonela's!

- ⚽ Soccer ball—on his prized left leg, of course. No explanation needed here.

- ⚽ Number 10, on his leg—his Barça and Argentina national team jersey number.

- ⚽ Mateo, on Leo's arm—the name of his second son.

BUY THIS! BRANDS LEO PROMOTES

Leo sells more than just soccer brilliance. Here are some of the brands he slaps his face and name on.

- Adidas—Leo promotes their soccer cleats and sports shirts and shorts.

- Tata—never heard of this Indian car company? Millions around the world have and more will, thanks to Leo.

- Pepsi—pass a fizzy drink this way, please.

- Gatorade—Leo's keeping with the sweet beverage theme.

- ⚽ Huawei—this Chinese telecom giant is even bigger after landing Leo as a spokesperson.

- ⚽ Lay's—Leo shot a commercial showing happy fans stealing his potato chips.

- ⚽ Louis Vuitton—Leo's very at home with this luxury fashion brand.

- ⚽ Mastercard—Leo's partnered with the credit card company since 2018.

- ⚽ Gillette—Messi shot a funny commercial with Roger Federer about Gillette razors that transform you into athletes from around the world.

- ⚽ SilkSilk—Messi gladly models for this fashion brand with a collection headed by his little sister, María.

FUN FACT

Leo's nickname is La Pugla,
which means "The Flea" in Spanish.
He got this nickname thanks to
his small stature and high speed.
It started as a family name, but
now the whole world knows
the GOAT is La Pugla!

CHAPTER 8

The GOAT Forever

Leo was thrilled. The world was thrilled. But back at Paris Saint-Germain, all was not well. In late April 2023, Leo went on a trip to Saudi Arabia. He missed a practice, and the team officials decided to suspend him for two weeks. Leo insisted that he didn't know he'd miss a practice by going on the trip, but the suspension left sour feelings between Leo and the club. Leo's contract with PSG was almost up and Leo and the team hadn't been able to reach a deal for a new one. Leo's heart wasn't on the PSG field, and when he played his last game on June 2, 2023, he was ready to go.

But Leo wasn't leaving the soccer field. He was just changing locations—and continents. On June 7, 2023, five days after his last PSG match, Leo thrilled American fans by announcing that he had signed with the MLS team Inter Miami CF. His two-and-a-half-year contract would last through 2025 and pay him 150 million dollars.

On July 16, Leo officially joined the Miami team roster and donned his pink, polo-collared jersey. And his explosive on-field presence has catapulted the club to a new level. In eleven games, Leo scored 14 goals. Attendance and merch sales at the games have gone up—way up. "We are talking about the best player of all time," Inter Miami coach Xavier Asensi said in an interview. "It's like being able to say you've seen Tiger Woods

play, or Michael Phelps swim, or Usain Bolt run, or watch Michael Jordan or Tom Brady."

The United States has embraced Leo. He was named the 2023 Most Valuable Player by Major League Soccer and *Time* magazine's 2023 Athlete of the Year. American celebrities and athletes have been just as thrilled as regular fans. Kim Kardashian, LeBron James, and Serena Williams have all been in the stands when Leo has taken the field. Kansas City Chiefs quarterback Patrick Mahomes—who plays a different kind of football—even got to meet Leo in a hallway before a match. "He's going to warm up," Patrick said in an interview. "What am I supposed to say? (I said) 'Have fun out there' and he had a goal and an assist, so I feel like he had a great time, he had fun, it was all on me."

Leo is in a good place. He likes his team and his family likes Miami. He's glad to be playing in the United States. And he's the same cool,

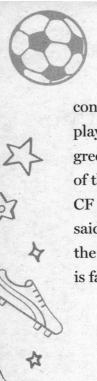

consistent phenom he's always been, whether playing in the dusty streets of Rosario, on the green field at Camp Nou, or under the glare of the Miami sun. His commitment to Miami CF will end when he's thirty-eight. Leo hasn't said yet what his plans will be afterward, but the world can be assured—Leo's life in soccer is far from over.

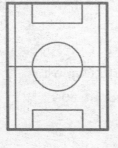

Leo vs. Ronaldo Showdown

Two of the greatest soccer players in the world go head-to-head in this matchup.

LEO
Birthday: June 24, 1987
Hometown: Rosario, Argentina
First pro soccer team: FC Barcelona
Pro soccer debut: October 16, 2004, age 17
Number of World Cup appearances: 5
Number of World Cup wins: 1
Career goals scored: 800+
Ballon d'Or won: 8
Number of career red cards: 3
Currently lives in: Giant mansion, Miami, Florida
Currently plays for: Inter Miami CF
Favorite food: His mom's chicken Milanesa
Gets around town driving: Oh, just a Maserati
Facial hair count: 0 mustaches, 1 beard

RONALDO

Birthday: February 5, 1985
Hometown: Funchal, Portugal
First pro soccer team: Sporting Clube de Portugal
Pro soccer debut: September 29, 2002, age 17
Number of World Cup appearances: 5
Number of World Cup wins: 0
Career goals scored: 800+
Ballon d'Or won: 5
Number of career red cards: 12
Currently lives in: Four Seasons hotel, Riyadh, Saudi Arabia
Currently plays for: Al-Nassr FC
Favorite food: Bacalhau à Brás, a salty Portuguese fish dish made with eggs, onions, and potatoes
Gets around town driving: One from his collection of twenty luxury cars
Facial hair count: 0 mustaches, 0 beards

In 2023, Ronaldo told the press that the rivalry was over. "Those who like Cristiano Ronaldo don't have to hate Messi and vice versa," he said to ESPN. "We've done well, we have changed the history of football … The legacy lives on, but I don't see the rivalry like that. We shared the stage many times . . . we're professional colleagues and we respect each other."

LEO SPEAKS

Leo mainly speaks with his feet—here, though, he weighs in with words.

 "This is for you, Diego."
—dedicating his eighth Ballon d'Or to the legendary Argentina player

 "I like everything sweet. I'm in love with it."
—Leo on his sweet tooth

 "Having a good World Cup is finishing in the top four, to be among the best four. At the very least, Argentina deserves to be there because of its history. Although it took a lot to get there, we have to get to it again."
—after the 2018 World Cup

"After winning the World Cup and not being able to go to Barça, it was time to go to the American league to experience football in a different way and enjoy the day-to-day."

"Today 95% or 100% of Argentin[eans] love me and that's a beautiful feeling."

"I want to be remembered as a good person, not only as a good football player."

"Look at this Cup, it's beautiful. We suffered a lot but we made it."
—after the 2022 World Cup

"It doesn't change anything for me to be the best or not . . . And I never tried to be, either."

"The road can be hard, but you have to keep fighting for your dreams to try to achieve them."

FUN FACT

Leo's older two sons, Thiago and Mateo, already play soccer, following in their dad's footsteps. The baby, Ciro? His sport of choice has yet to be decided!

LEO THROUGH TIME

April 2024

Leo is named the MLS Player of the Month.

2023

Leo leaves Paris Saint-Germain and joins Inter Miami CF in the United States, thrilling American soccer fans. He is chosen as *Time* magazine's Athlete of the Year and wins his eighth Ballon d'Or, more than any other current player.

2022

Leo wins his first World Cup in a final match against France, ending the game with a heart-stopping penalty kick shoot-out.

2021

Rocking the soccer world, Leo announces he's leaving FC Barcelona and signing with the French club Paris Saint-Germain.

2019

Leo and Antonela's third son, Ciro, is born.

2017

Leo and Antonela get married in Rosario.

2016

Leo and his father, Jorge, are convicted of tax fraud in a Spanish court and ordered to pay fines.

2015

Mateo is born. He is Leo and Antonela's second son.

2014

Leo plays for Argentina in the World Cup in Brazil. He misses a goal in the final game, and Argentina loses 1–0 to Germany.

2012

Thiago, Leo's first son with his girlfriend, Antonela, is born.

2009

Leo is awarded his first Ballon d'Or, the top individual soccer award in Europe, one of eight he will eventually receive.

2006

Leo plays for Argentina in his first World Cup in Germany—and scores a goal!

2005

Leo scores his first official goal with FC Barcelona and receives Spanish citizenship, clearing his way to continue playing for the team.

2001

Leo and his family move from Argentina to Barcelona so Leo can play for FC Barcelona. But the move is not a happy one, and Leo's mother and siblings eventually move back to Argentina.

2000

Leo tries out for FC Barcelona's youth academy team and is signed in December.

1998

Leo is diagnosed with the medical condition growth hormone deficiency. He learns to give himself shots so he will grow taller.

1994

Leo joins the local youth soccer team, Newell's Old Boys.

June 24, 1987

Leo is born in Rosario, Argentina.